1400208

629.45
Lan   Langille, Jacque-
         line

         The space shuttle

DUE DATE	BRODART	10/01	5.95

Space Shuttle, The

Jacqueline Langille

Lex: 900   RL: 3.5   GRL: Pts: 3

Eye on the Universe

The Space Shuttle

USA

NASA Endeavour

Jacqueline Langille & Bobbie Kalman

Crabtree Publishing Company

www.crabtreebooks.com

Eye on the Universe

Created by Bobbie Kalman

For Daniel Arseneault,
to the Moon and back

Editor-in-Chief
Bobbie Kalman

Writing team
Jacqueline Langille
Bobbie Kalman

Managing editor
Lynda Hale

Editors
April Fast
Heather Levigne

Computer design
Lynda Hale
Lucy DeFazio
Campbell Creative Services

Production coordinator
Hannelore Sotzek

Special thanks to
NASA

Photographs
NASA: pages 11 (both), 12, 14 (bottom), 14-15, 16, 17, 18, 19,
    20, 21, 22 (bottom), 23 (both), 24, 30
Photo Researchers, Inc./NASA/Science Photo Library: pages 22 (top),
    25 (top), 31
Photo Researchers, Inc./NASA/Science Source: page 25 (bottom)
Photri, Inc.: pages 8, 9
Other photographs by Digital Stock and Digital Vision

Illustrations
Barbara Bedell: page 13
Cori Marvin: page 6

Printer
Worzalla Publishing Company

Color separations and film
Dot 'n Line Image Inc.

Crabtree Publishing Company

PMB 16A
350 Fifth Ave.,
Suite 3308
N.Y., N.Y. 10118

612 Welland Ave.,
St. Catharines,
Ontario, Canada
L2M 5V6

73 Lime Walk
Headington
Oxford OX3 7AD
United Kingdom

Cataloging in Publication Data
Langille, Jacqueline
    The space shuttle

(Eye on the universe)
Includes index.

ISBN 0-86505-678-1 (library bound)   ISBN 0-86505-688-9 (pbk.)
This book describes the construction and operation of NASA's space
shuttles, covering such topics as preparation for liftoff, living in space,
landing, and mission control.

1. Space shuttles—United States—Juvenile literature. 2. Space Shuttle
Program (U.S.)—Juvenile literature. [1. Space shuttles.] I. Kalman, Bobbie.
II. Title. III. Series: Kalman, Bobbie. Eye on the universe.

TL795.5.L36 1998   j629.45 21   LC 98-3682
                                                                        CIP

Contents

What is the space shuttle?

The **space shuttle** is a vehicle used to transport people into space and then bring them back to Earth. The United States' space agency, called **NASA**, has four space shuttles in use: Columbia, Atlantis, Discovery, and Endeavour. Spacecraft that orbit, or travel around, Earth when they are in space are also called **orbiters**.

The reusable "space plane"

Most types of spacecraft go into space once and stay for a long time. If they come back to Earth, they burn up in the air or crash on the ground. Shuttles are different from other spacecraft because they are reusable—they can go into space more than once.

Space shuttles are built to fly up to 100 **missions**, or space flights. At the end of a mission, they leave space and come back to Earth. They land on a runway in almost the same way an airplane lands after a flight. Space Shuttle Discovery, shown right, is almost ready for liftoff.

A closer look

The space shuttle system includes four parts: the orbiter spacecraft, two **solid rocket boosters** or **SRB**s, and an **external fuel tank**. The SRBs and the three main engines on the orbiter provide the **thrust**, or force, needed to take the shuttle into space. The large external tank holds the fuel for the main engines. The external fuel tank is not reusable because it breaks up and falls into the ocean. The SRBs can be reused many times. (See page 13.)

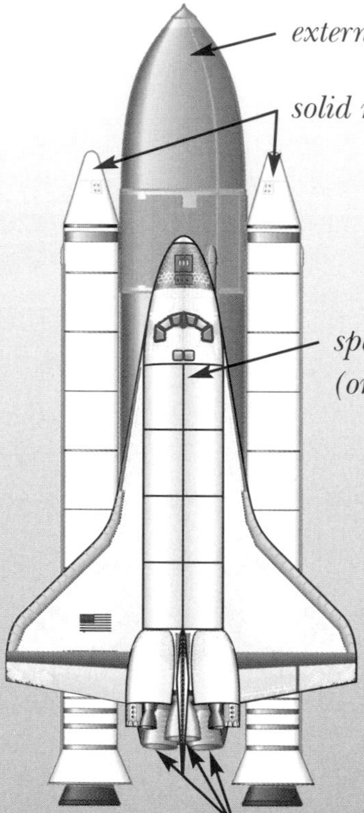

external fuel tank

solid rocket boosters

space shuttle (orbiter)

three main engines

Inside the forward section of the shuttle

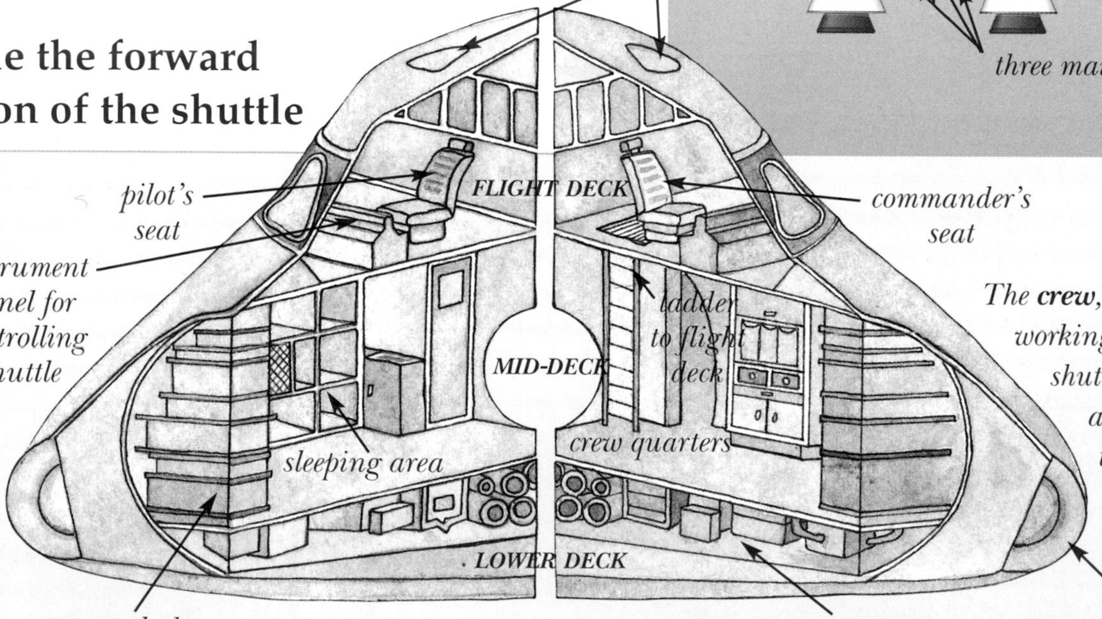

overhead windows

pilot's seat

FLIGHT DECK

commander's seat

instrument panel for controlling shuttle

ladder to flight deck

MID-DECK

The crew, or the people working aboard the shuttle, eat, sleep, and live in the crew quarters.

sleeping area

crew quarters

storage lockers

LOWER DECK

storage area

nose of shuttle

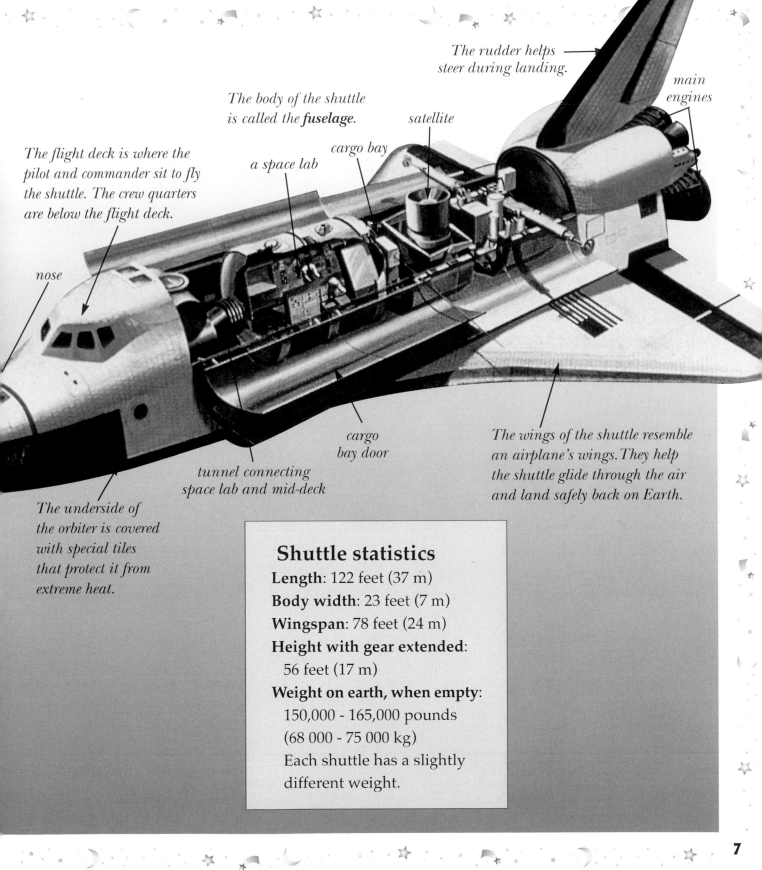

The rudder helps steer during landing.

main engines

The body of the shuttle is called the **fuselage**.

satellite

cargo bay

The flight deck is where the pilot and commander sit to fly the shuttle. The crew quarters are below the flight deck.

a space lab

nose

The underside of the orbiter is covered with special tiles that protect it from extreme heat.

tunnel connecting space lab and mid-deck

cargo bay door

The wings of the shuttle resemble an airplane's wings. They help the shuttle glide through the air and land safely back on Earth.

Shuttle statistics

Length: 122 feet (37 m)
Body width: 23 feet (7 m)
Wingspan: 78 feet (24 m)
Height with gear extended:
   56 feet (17 m)
Weight on earth, when empty:
   150,000 - 165,000 pounds
   (68 000 - 75 000 kg)
   Each shuttle has a slightly
   different weight.

Preparing for a mission

Thousands of people at the Kennedy Space Center in Cape Canaveral, Florida, help prepare a shuttle for a mission. Before the orbiter is ready for the **launch**, or liftoff, people check all its parts to make sure they are working properly and safely. The cargo bay is loaded, and the equipment for the mission is put into the orbiter. Food and other supplies are stored on board.

Putting it all together

The SRBs and a new, gigantic external tank arrive at the **Vehicle Assembly Building**, or **VAB**, about six months before the mission date. Each SRB is in four pieces. They are put together inside the 50-story VAB.

The orbiter is **mated**, or connected, to the SRBs and external fuel tank 41 days before the mission. Putting the **Space Transportation System**, or **STS**, together takes from four to six weeks. It is assembled inside the VAB. When the shuttle is finally mated and ready to be launched, its nose points toward the sky.

(left) The protective tiles are carefully checked after each mission. Many are replaced before the shuttle is ready to go into space again. Each tile is made to fit one particular place on the shuttle's body. Even a tiny crack in one tile could endanger the lives of the crew on their return to Earth.

(right) Each section of Space Shuttle Columbia is checked thoroughly before its next voyage. The work is done in the Vehicle Assembly Building.

Checking the lists

All repairs and preparations must be carefully checked before the launch. Each person working on a job goes over a checklist before the job is finished. Making sure the jobs have been inspected helps keep the shuttle safe.

Before the launch

For most missions, the countdown to liftoff begins three days before the launch. A huge machine called a **crawler** slowly takes the shuttle from the VAB to the **launch pad**, the area from which the shuttle lifts off. Many jobs must be done in a certain order during the countdown. The countdown is stopped at certain times to allow things to be fixed and double-checked. When only one hour and 40 minutes remain in the countdown, the crew boards the shuttle.

*The objects and materials that are carried in the cargo bay are the shuttle's **payload**, or cargo. Spacecraft called **satellites** are the usual payload. Other countries often pay NASA to put their satellites into orbit. The shuttle carries up to 65,000 pounds (29 484 kg) of cargo. The cargo in this picture is a space lab on Orbiter Columbia. The workers wear blue suits over their clothes to make sure everything stays very clean inside the shuttle.*

The crawler makes its slow journey from the Vehicle Assembly Building to the launch pad, which can be seen at the top of this large photograph. The smaller picture shows the crawler as it reaches the launch pad.

Ready for blastoff!

Before the launch, the crew members are strapped into **accelerator seats**, which help them stay in place. They are now ready for liftoff! When the engines start, the shuttle begins to shake. The crew members hear a loud roar from the rocket boosters as the shuttle lifts off the launch pad. Once they are in the air, they feel as though they are on a giant roller coaster that is climbing higher and higher. They then feel a heavy weight on their body, called the "g"-force, caused by traveling at increasing speeds. In space, the heavy feeling disappears because they travel at one steady speed.

*At liftoff, the three main engines and the SRBs thrust Space Shuttle Discovery into the air. The rocket boosters continue to **fire**, or burn fuel, for about two minutes before they separate from the shuttle and fall into the ocean (shown right). After nine minutes, the external fuel tank comes off the orbiter and falls back to Earth. (See illustration on page 13.) The fuel tank breaks up into small pieces that fall into the ocean. The orbiter then continues its journey into space. Two smaller engines move it around while it is on orbit.*

external tank

rocket boosters

A robotic arm lifts the payload out of the cargo bay, and the orbiter moves away.

Mission Control

Launch Operations at Kennedy Space Center looks after the preparations that take place before the launch. After liftoff, Mission Control at the Johnson Space Center in Houston takes over until the shuttle returns to Earth. Mission Control workers use video cameras, satellites, radios, and computers to communicate with the shuttle crew.

To ensure a safe trip, Mission Control watches over everything that happens on the shuttle. If the crew needs help with a problem or job, they can speak directly to an expert on Earth.

One of the video screens shows three crew members on Space Shuttle Discovery giving a television interview. The middle screen shows the shuttle passing over Mexico.

Flight controllers

Hundreds of people work at Mission Control in Texas. Good teamwork between the people on the ground and the crew on the shuttle make a mission successful. The people who talk directly to the crew members and guide them in their mission are called **flight controllers**. They direct the entire day for the crew and even wake them up in the morning with music. The flight controllers try to pick an upbeat or funny song to put the shuttle crew members in a good mood.

Mission Control constantly receives information from the orbiter's computers. Some of the information is used right away to check how the shuttle is working. Other information is gathered together and studied later. It helps the flight controllers study the overall mission.

The people on board

The crew members aboard the shuttle are called **astronauts**. Astronaut means "star sailor." Some astronauts, such as the pilot, have special training to fly the orbiter. Others are scientists who work on experiments in space. Experiments help scientists figure out problems or discover new facts about space. Only two crew members, the commander and the pilot, are needed to take the shuttle into space and bring it back to Earth. For each mission, however, between two and seven astronauts travel in the orbiter.

Joining the crew

Only people with a university or college degree in engineering, science, or mathematics can become astronauts. They must also be very healthy! Every two years, NASA chooses about 100 men and women for a one-year training program. The trainees who finish the program then become astronauts. In 1995, Lieutenant Colonel Eileen Collins was the first female to pilot a space shuttle. In 1998, she became the first female commander of a shuttle mission.

(left) ***Mission specialists***, *such as astronaut Robert Curbeam, Jr., make sure work on the shuttle goes smoothly.* ***Payload crew members***, *including the payload commander, are scientists who run the experiments. Payload specialists do not take part in the astronaut-training program.*

(opposite) These crew members on ***STS-9***, *which is the code name for the ninth shuttle mission, show off a little for the camera. They show that "up" and "down" have no meaning in space.*

Living in space

Gravity is a force that pulls objects to the center of a planet or moon. Earth's gravity pulls on the Space Shuttle, keeping it on orbit around the planet. The force of Earth's gravity affects the Space Shuttle's crew differently when they are in space than when they are on the ground. In space, people feel weightless, and everything floats in **microgravity**. All loose objects must be tied down with straps or attached to a wall with Velcro®. To keep tools from floating away, astronauts attach them to their belt using Velcro® strips.

How do they go?

In microgravity, going to the bathroom is not easy! The toilets on the shuttle are like the ones on Earth, but in space, astronauts must put their feet in holders, tie on a seat belt, and use handrails.

To get rid of urine, they use a tube with a plastic cup on the end. Before the mission, a special cup is made to fit each crew member. Urine goes through the tube and into the toilet. A fan on the toilet uses air to draw the wastes into storage tanks.

Every activity that seems easy on Earth can be difficult in microgravity. Even combing hair is a challenge. Hair floats away from an astronaut's head but, at least, it does not tangle much. Being in space gives "a bad-hair day" brand-new meaning!

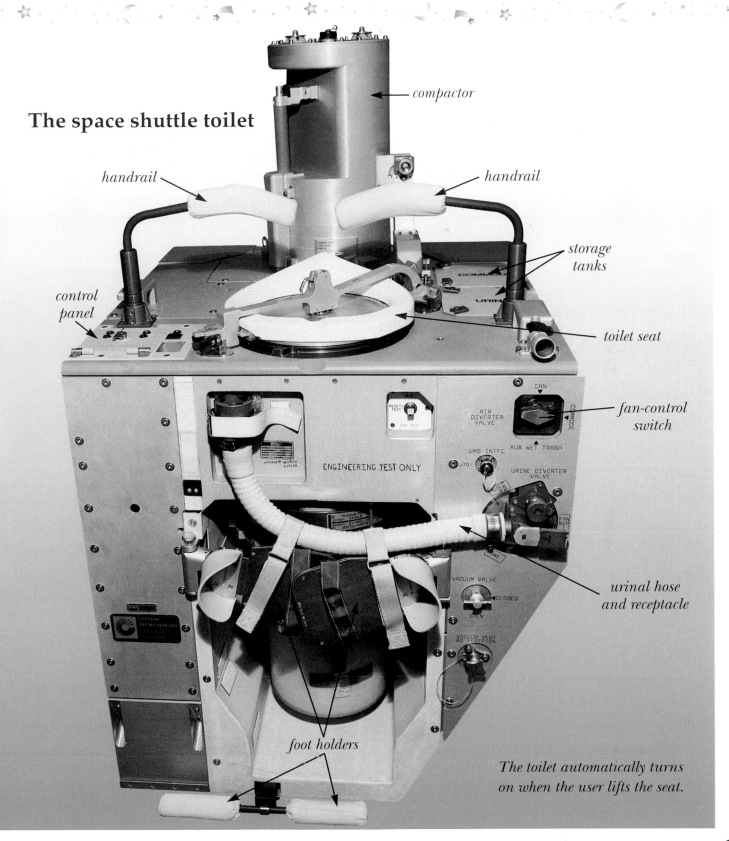

The space shuttle toilet

compactor

handrail

handrail

storage tanks

control panel

toilet seat

fan-control switch

ENGINEERING TEST ONLY

urinal hose and receptacle

foot holders

The toilet automatically turns on when the user lifts the seat.

Mealtime

On Earth, people store food and make meals using refrigerators and stoves. The shuttle has no room for large refrigerators and stoves. Even if it did have room, these appliances would use up the power needed for shuttle work. Most shuttle food is precooked on Earth and stored in special containers that keep it fresh. After it is cooked, the food is cut into bite-sized pieces and **freeze-dried**. In freeze-drying, all the liquid is removed as the food is quickly frozen. Before astronauts eat, they **rehydrate**, or add water to the food.

Eating in space

Meals are prepared in the orbiter kitchen, which is called a **galley**. For each meal, the astronauts take turns preparing the food. Food preparation takes about 30 minutes. A meal is placed on a food tray that straps onto a crew member's legs. Packaged food is tied down to the tray, and a knife, spoon, and fork are connected with Velcro®. Most foods have sauces that make them hold together in microgravity. These foods are easier to eat because they stick to the fork or spoon.

The astronauts use a food warmer to heat their food. Even though it can be eaten cold, they say warm food tastes better. Crew members have to be careful, especially when eating with chopsticks, because microgravity can cause food to float away. Tiny drops of liquid or pieces of food can get inside shuttle equipment and cause problems.

Sample menu

Breakfast
applesauce
beef jerky
granola
breakfast roll
chocolate instant breakfast
orange-grapefruit drink

Lunch
corned beef
asparagus
two pieces of bread
pears
peanuts
two lemonade drinks

Dinner
beef with barbecue sauce
cauliflower with cheese
green beans with mushrooms
lemon pudding
pecan cookies
cocoa

Condiments: ketchup, hot sauce, salt and pepper (in liquid form), mustard, mayonnaise

A day on the shuttle

The astronauts are very busy aboard the shuttle. They often work 16 hours a day in order to complete all the projects set out for the mission. Every activity the crew needs to do is listed on a daily plan called a **Payload Crew Activity Plan** or **PCAP**.

The PCAP guides the crew members through each minute of every day. Besides eating and working, the crew members also have to exercise regularly. Exercise is necessary to keep the astronauts healthy in microgravity.

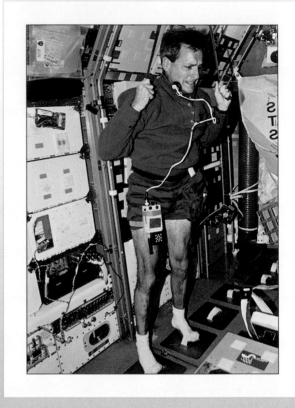

(above) This astronaut is exercising his muscles by pulling down on thick rubber bands. His feet are strapped to the floor.

(left) Astronauts cannot take showers because water floats in microgravity. Tiny drops of water could drift away and damage the shuttle's equipment. Instead, they clean themselves with a wet and soapy cloth and then towel dry. Crew members wash their hair with rinseless shampoo and dry it with a towel.

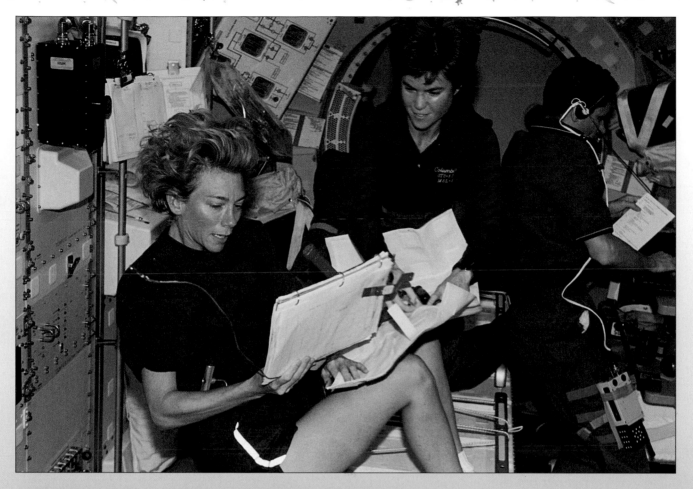

(above) The pilot, left, and the payload commander, center, review notes during a daily planning session. Another astronaut works on a laptop computer.

(left) The astronauts sleep in their seat or tie themselves to the wall of the shuttle. On some missions, the crew uses beds, which are called **sleep stations**. These beds are hard, but in microgravity they feel soft. The crew members usually strap themselves into special bags, called **sleep restraints**. Sleep restraints keep them from floating around and bumping into walls or equipment inside the orbiter.

Working on board

From space, astronauts study the geography, pollution, and weather patterns on Earth. They take many photographs to record their observations. Planets and stars are also easier to study from the shuttle. Astronauts **conduct**, or work on, experiments to learn how space conditions, such as microgravity, affect humans, animals, plants, and insects.

A laboratory in space

Scientists and engineers from all over the world work together in a space laboratory, or lab, filled with computers, workbenches, and scientific equipment.

The people who work in a space lab are payload specialists. Their only job is to conduct experiments.

Some experiments are conducted inside the lab and some outside the shuttle on open **pallets**, or racks. A space lab is used only when scientists need extra room to work. It does not go on every mission, however.

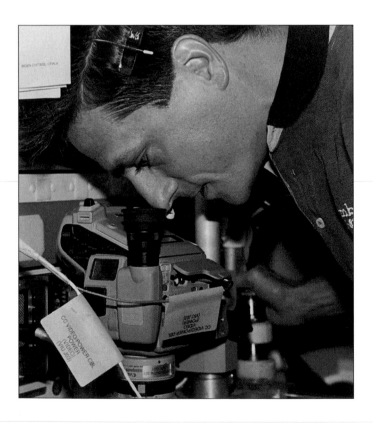

*On STS-94, astronaut Donald Thomas, a mission specialist, observes an experiment through the eyepiece of a **camcorder**, which is a small video camera. He records his observations on tape so that they can be studied on Earth after the mission is finished.*

(above) The experiments conducted by these payload specialists aboard Columbia are inside **gloveboxes**, which keep out germs and prevent spilling. They are sealed on all sides and have windows so the scientists can see the experiment inside.

(left) This picture of the Southern Lights, or **Aurora Australis**, was taken from the flight deck. Photographs of Earth taken from the shuttle help scientists learn more about the planet.

Working outside

Astronauts sometimes go outside the orbiter to work. Working outside is called **extra-vehicular activity** or **EVA**. To get ready for EVA, an astronaut goes into the **airlock**, which is a large metal drum with a door on either end. Astronauts prepare for an EVA inside the airlock. When they are ready to go out, all the air is released from the airlock and the outside **hatch**, or door, is opened. Without the airlock, each crew member would have to put on a special suit whenever an astronaut went outside.

Going out alone

In the past, astronauts had to stay connected to their spacecraft by a long line called a **tether**. Today, they can use a machine called a **Manned Maneuvering Unit** or **MMU** to move freely outside the shuttle. The MMU looks like a large armchair. It is strapped to an astronaut's back, and he or she moves around using controls on the armrest. An astronaut on the MMU makes repairs to satellites or brings them into the cargo bay.

*While astronauts work outside the shuttle, they stay in contact with the crew inside using a microphone and headphones. This equipment is attached to a **Snoopy cap** that they wear under their helmet.*

A space suit is necessary for working outside the shuttle. It is made from a strong material that resists tearing caused by tiny space particles called **micrometeors**. It also protects the astronauts from the radiation of the Sun. Heating and cooling systems in the space suit keep the astronauts from feeling the extreme heat and cold. The airtight suits also have a six to eight hour oxygen supply.

The orbiter in action

Once it is in space, the orbiter serves as a base to **deploy**, or send out, payloads such as satellites or space probes. Satellites that need to be repaired or serviced can be brought on board and later released back into space or returned to Earth. Each satellite costs millions of dollars, so it is much less expensive to repair damaged equipment than to replace it.

What an arm!

Astronauts use an **RMS**, or **Remote Manipulator System**, to help them do certain jobs outside the shuttle. The RMS is a robot arm that an astronaut controls from inside the orbiter. It "grabs" objects in space and puts them into the payload bay. The RMS also carries astronauts back and forth between the orbiter and other spacecraft. Cameras are located in the payload bay and on the RMS. They help the astronauts see exactly what the RMS is doing as they guide its movements.

*(left) Orbiter Atlantis is attached to the Mir Space Station. Joining together two or more spacecraft in orbit is called **docking**. Orbiters like Atlantis are the "trucks" of outer space. They bring supplies such as food and equipment to the space station. They also transport astronauts to and from Mir.*

(opposite) Two astronauts guide a satellite into the payload bay for repairs. The long, white RMS on the right helps catch the satellite and bring it in close to the shuttle. Repairing and reusing satellites cuts down on space garbage.

Landing the space shuttle

When the mission is over, the crew members get ready to return to Earth. They pack up the equipment and strap themselves into their seats. They are now prepared to leave orbit. Leaving orbit is also called **re-entry** because the shuttle re-enters the **atmosphere**. The atmosphere is the blanket of air that surrounds Earth. Small engines called **thrusters** turn the shuttle so that it begins to head back toward Earth. The shuttle does not use its engines to come in for a landing. It glides through the atmosphere.

Slowing down to land

As the shuttle gets closer to Earth, the atmosphere gets thicker. **Friction**, or air rubbing against the shuttle, slows down the orbiter and makes it very hot. It is still going too fast to land, however. To slow it down even more, the commander guides it through some big S-shaped turns. The pilots have only one chance to get the speed right. A **drag parachute** also opens to slow down the shuttle. When the shuttle lands, the brakes on the **landing-gear** wheels bring it to a complete stop.

(left) After landing, the astronauts remain in Space Shuttle Atlantis for several minutes. The outside of the shuttle is very hot and there might be poisonous or explosive fuel left in the engine.

(right) The drag parachute opens at the back of the shuttle to steady the aircraft, slow it down, and help reduce the wear on the brakes.

The Challenger disaster

People at the VAB, Kennedy Space Center, and Mission Control work very hard to make a mission successful, but sometimes accidents happen. In 1986, Orbiter Challenger was destroyed shortly after liftoff. An **O-ring seal**, which keeps gases from leaking through metal parts on a shuttle, failed to work properly. An explosion tore apart the shuttle, and seven people were killed, including a school teacher named Christa McAuliffe.

After the Challenger disaster, scientists worked for two years to fix the O-ring problem. During that time, no space shuttles went into space. In 1988, Shuttle Discovery launched successfully, and the STS began operating again. Scientists are constantly working to ensure that transportation between Earth and space is safe. Shuttle Endeavour was completed in 1991 to replace Challenger and bring the number of orbiters back up to four.

Glossary

astronaut A person who is trained to fly or travel in a spacecraft

crawler A big vehicle that slowly moves the shuttle to the launch pad

flight deck The upper compartment in the forward part of the space shuttle

glovebox A box that is sealed on all sides and has windows for viewing experiments inside

gravity The force that pulls things toward the center of a planet or moon

microgravity Very little gravity; weightlessness

mission specialists Astronauts who are responsible for shuttle systems, crew activity planning, meals, and payload bay activity

orbit (v) To travel around a planet or star in space; (n) the path taken to travel around a planet or star

orbiter A spacecraft that orbits Earth

payload Cargo carried aboard the shuttle, such as a satellite

payload specialists Persons other than NASA astronauts who work in the laboratory aboard the orbiter

satellite An object that travels in a particular orbit around a body in space

Snoopy cap A snug-fitting cap with a microphone and headphones that astronauts wear under their helmet while working outside the shuttle in space

SRBs (solid rocket boosters) Tall, white, reusable rockets that launch the shuttle into space

space lab A scientific laboratory that is carried in the shuttle's cargo bay and used to conduct experiments in space

space shuttle A spacecraft used to transport people into space and bring them back to Earth

Index

4 5 6 7 8 9 0   Printed in the U.S.A.   7 6 5 4 3 2 1